# GRIEF 2 GROWTH

## PLANTED, NOT BURIED

### HOW TO SURVIVE & THRIVE
### AFTER LIFE'S GREATEST CHALLENGES

# BRIAN D. SMITH

# GRIEF 2 GROWTH

# Table of Contents

# TABLE OF CONTENTS

# INTRODUCTION

In this book I will explore what grief is, what you can expect while in grief, and how you can best cope with the universal human experience of grief. Grief is not an emotion, grief is a container for a myriad of emotions that ebb and flow (credit to R. Glenn Kelly for this insight). I will talk about what some of those emotions are and bust some myths about grief.

If you know someone in grief, hopefully you'll find something here that will help you understand what they are going through and how you can help them navigate it. I'll talk about things you should and shouldn't say to the grieving and how you can help them. If you have purchased this for someone else, don't pass it along to them without reading it yourself.

For the grieving, I will tell you what you can do today to cope with grief and maintain some semblance of a "normal" life, while dealing with the early stages of grief which can be overwhelming. These are techniques that I found helped me four years ago when I found myself mired in a grief I thought I would not survive. They helped then. They help now.

In addition to practical daily tips, I will talk about a shift in perspective which I believe is the secret to transforming grief from something that could destroy you into something that you can use to grow, as insane as that might sound to you right now.

# CHAPTER 1
## WHAT IS GRIEF?

Grief is a universal human emotion. If you live long enough, you will experience grief. 100% of the people you love will die. You, will die. Everyone who is born dies. The only question is, "Will you grieve them or will they grieve you?" Yet, as universal as grief is, grief is not understood by many of us. We avoid talking about grief. Many of us cruise through life willfully unaware that grief is waiting for us.

The odds are that if you are reading this, it's because you are experiencing grief. It's also likely it has caught you off-guard. When grief strikes, we feel like we've been buried and our lives are over.

Grief is deep, prolonged mental anguish, intense sorrow, emotional suffering, resulting from a loss- especially from the death of a loved one. Grief manifests in many ways- Shock, disbelief, anger, rage, fear, sadness, uncontrollable crying, a feeling of emptiness, the belief life will never be the same again, the belief you will never be happy, a lack of concentration. Life feels like it's falling apart or has even come to a halt. We say things like "My world has ended."

Grief is the most painful human emotion possible.

# CHAPTER 2
## WHO IS THIS GUY?

Who am I? And, why should you believe I know anything worth saying about grief? In life, we can learn in one of two ways. We can learn through study or we can learn through experience. Many people call themselves experts because they have studied a subject intellectually. But, there is no teacher like experience. When it comes to grief, I have learned both ways- experientially and through study.

My fifteen-year-old daughter, Shayna, passed in her sleep on June 24, 2015. 1,361 days ago today. With each passing day, I become one day more experienced with grief. When it comes to grief, I have been there. I am there.

When Shayna passed, I threw myself into studying grief because that's what I do. I research things. I take them apart, analyze them, and put them back together. Early on in my journey, I found that there is a podcast for any subject in the world. One of the first podcasts I discovered  after Shayna's passing was "We Don't Die" by Sandra Champlain. It's at www.wedontdieradio.com. Sandra recorded an audio about grief that I listened to a few weeks after Shayna passed. That audio helped me immensely. Then, my wife and I listened to it together. Sandra's work, and the work of others, has inspired me.

My wife did more studying of grief than I did in terms of reading specifically about the subject of grief. Instead of studying grief, I poured myself into studies that would alleviate my grief, I studied anything that would bring me hope.

I didn't set out to become an expert in grief. I was trying to figure out how to conquer it.  I learned along the way that grief could not be conquered. But, it could be managed. I wouldn't put it behind me. However, it would not destroy me. I developed my own "program", if you will that helped me survive those days when I thought I would not survive.

That program is a combination of exercise, meditation, study, and service to others. I will share that with you.

BRIAN D. SMITH

# CHAPTER 3
## WHY DO WE GRIEVE?

Why do we grieve? If loss is a part of life; if death is normal, why do we mourn? I've heard grief described as being similar to withdrawal from drugs. We physically crave the person we are missing. Our brains have gotten used to their feel, their smell, everything about them. There is something their physical presence does for us that we become addicted to. When we lack that, it triggers a reaction, not unlike drug withdrawal. I believe there is something to this theory, but it doesn't explain everything associated with grief.

We don't grieve when people leave the house for a few hours, go on vacation, or even move for months or years at a time. We are just as separated from a loved one on a long trip as we are from a loved one separated by death. When they are on a trip, there is something about knowing they're OK and they will return that gives us comfort. We know the separation is temporary and we take solace in that. We miss them, but we don't grieve them. Grief happens when our mental image of what should be doesn't line up with what is. Grief happens when we lose hope of seeing them again.

There are 360,000 births and 150,000 deaths every day in the world. Both birth and death are common occurrences. We know that every person who is born will eventually die. Yet, death seems to shock us. Birth is celebrated. We invite others to participate in our joy of bringing a life into the world. We fear death. We avoid the very thought of it, until it comes. And then, often, we grieve alone.

## DEATH IS A STRANGER

There was a time when people saw death all the time. Growing up on a farm, people saw the natural cycles of life and death in the farm animals. People used to die at home surrounded by family instead of in hospitals or nursing homes. After death, the body would be kept at home until the burial. Now, death is hidden away. Bodies are quickly whisked off and handled by professionals. Most of us have never seen a person die.

We think death is what happens to other families. When death comes to one of our loved ones, we are unprepared. After the passing of a loved one friends and families often avoid us as if death is contagious. Because we are so uncomfortable with death, what it is, and the fact that it's inevitable, we grieve harder than we need to.

## KNOWLEDGE IS POWER

The more we know about a condition like grief, the better we can cope with it. Death is an unpleasant subject. Grief is an uncomfortable subject. So, we tend to avoid both. Lack of knowledge leads to fear. Fear keeps us from seeking knowledge. The fear and ignorance play off of each other in a destructive cycle. We put off things like buying life insurance, funeral planning,  and preparing a will as if they will cause a death.

Parents don't expect their children to pass before them. We are particularly unprepared for the loss of a child. We would like to believe this is something that never happens. I certainly felt both my girls would live longer than me, even though my father's mother lost two children before the ages of twenty-two.

You might be surprised to learn that for people over fifty years old almost 12% have lost a child. For black people, this figure is nearly 17%. For white people, it's roughly 10%. One in eight people over the age of fifty will has lost a child. Even if your child is ill for a prolonged period and you know she's going to pass, you spend time caring for her, not studying grief. There's the anticipatory grief you have to deal with before her crossing. Then, there's the grief after. Learning about grief while we're grieving is difficult. Our brain is rewiring itself during this time. Our brain chemistry is out of balance Grief causes short-term brain damage. Grief has a tremendous impact on the memory, learning, perception, and communication areas of the brain. It's difficult to concentrate. It's nearly impossible to retain things.

For many people, reading is painfully difficult. Without the ability to focus and remember, we will read paragraphs or even pages and not remember what we just read immediately after. Sometimes we will have to read and re-read a passage and still have difficulty retaining it. We operate in a fog. It's for that reason, I am presenting this in audio form as well as in a text format. Grief skews our perception of what is going on around us. We become hypersensitive. We often project bad intentions into other people's actions. This can cause fights among families. If a sibling wants a piece of Mom's jewelry, we might see them as greedy; when during any other time we would see they simply want a keepsake.

Educating ourselves about grief can help us cope with it. For me, actively dealing with my pain was the only way to go. I immediately immersed myself into studying and actively confronting the grief. I read, listened to, and viewed everything I could find. Later, I will share some coping mechanisms that worked for me. Learning that the feelings I was having were "normal" relieved the isolation. Friends were OK, but

I needed new friends. People who hadn't gone through what I was going through could never understand. Surrounding myself with people who were one year, two years, ten years into their grief gave me hope. I modeled my life on theirs, and I thought "If they can do it, I can do it."

# CHAPTER 4
## WHAT TO EXPECT IN GRIEF

### NUMBNESS

During the early stages of grief, you might notice you can't feel, and have the concern that you will never feel again. This emotional numbness is normal and will pass. This emotional anesthesia is a protection provided by shock because you cannot handle everything at once. You probably have responsibilities like funeral arrangements to get through. You very well might go on auto-pilot and continue to function "normally' until you can't anymore. You'll hit a wall. You might not cry at the funeral and wonder what is wrong with you. In these early stages, you can even feel guilty because you don't think you are grieving enough. "How can I eat when she's dead? How can I sleep when she's not here?" The reality is you have to, for your other loved ones and for yourself. You are doing what you need to do.

Patience is key. Grief will take a while to process. Working on your grief can make it bearable and progress faster. But, working on your grief will not cure it overnight. Grief will be a companion for a while. Don't try to rush it away.

## DEATH WISH AND SUICIDAL THOUGHTS

When you're grieving, you might find you want to die. In my case, it was my daughter that I lost. When you lose someone that close to you, someone you're responsible for, someone who was supposed to live long beyond your years, it's natural to want to be with them. And, since you feel it is death that is separating you, it's only your death that can bring you back together. If it's a small child, you might feel you need to be with them to take care of them. At 15 years old, I knew where Shayna was every day and every night.

I was responsible for her well-being. I wanted to be with her where she was, after her passing.

I have talked to hundreds of parents since then. While this is something most will not admit openly for fear of being thought "crazy," my anecdotal experience is the majority of parents who have lost children at some point have suicidal thoughts or at least wish to die to be with their child. I recall the first time I heard a parent admit this. I was in the car listening to a podcast when I heard her say that a bus was driving by and she felt the urge to step out in front of it. She had written a book. I immediately knew I had to get that book. Just knowing someone else felt the way I did, made my feelings seem not as bad. While driving, I had images of slamming my car into a bridge abutment or head-on into oncoming traffic.

I didn't seriously consider suicide or make plans for it. I had fleeting thoughts. But, the desire to be with Shayna continues four years after her passing. Every morning I wake up, I think "Here I am again."; and not in a rejoicing tone. Every day I count as one day closer to our reunion. If you're fixating on suicidal thoughts or find yourself planning suicide, it's time to get help. But, if you have those random thoughts or you find yourself longing to be with your loved one, you're not alone, and you're not crazy.

## INDIFFERENCE

Grief can lead to feeling indifferent. This is slightly different from numbness from emotion. You will possibly stop caring about things, maybe even loved ones. You might let go of things you need to do. You might stop getting dressed. You might not pay bills. You might start missing work or appointments. Feeling like you couldn't control the passing of your loved one might lead to the feeling you can't control anything. And, in comparison, these routine cares of the world don't matter. Suicidal feelings can arise. Dangerous behavior can ensue, as you don't care about your own safety. When your indifference causes you to put yourself or others into danger, it's time to seek help.

## CLINGING TO THE PAST

When you lose a loved one, you might cling to their possessions. People often ask when they should change their child's room or when they should get rid of their loved one's clothes. The answer is "Whenever it's right for you." People might encourage you to "let go". Only you can say when that time is right. Clinging to their possessions might give you a sense of control. It might make you feel like you are keeping them with you. There is absolutelys nothing wrong with keepsakes. However, hopefully soon you'll come to the realization you don't need their possessions to keep them with you. They're here whether their stuff is or not.

## GUILT OR REGRET

After the passing of a loved one, guilt is also common. You will find reasons to blame yourself, even well beyond any reasonable expectations. "I should have been there." "I shouldn't have let her go alone." "I should have seen signs." "Why wasn't I there when she passed?"

Just yesterday, I heard someone say we should live like every day is our last. That's nonsense. We can't live like every day will be our last. If I thought the Tuesday before Shayna passed would be the last day for either of us, I wouldn't have left the house without her. We don't always part as if we'll never see our loved ones again. It's not possible or desirable to live that way. Every night I told Shayna I loved her and I kissed her on the cheek. That last night, she was in her bathroom getting ready for bed when I came upstairs. I told her I loved her through the door. I did not kiss her. I don't allow that to haunt me. She knows I love her and I kissed her plenty.

I gave Shayna an injection every other week for her rheumatoid arthritis. When she passed I wondered if I had somehow messed up the shot and killed her. It was an absurd thought. But, it persisted for a couple of weeks.

I wondered if we had missed something with her medical history. Should I have taken her to a different cardiologist? Should I have been more aggressive with her treatment of what we were told was a mild non-life-threatening condition? I had taken her to one of the best cardiologists in the country. We did two aggressive procedures on her even though he said they were not necessary. Still, the guilt tried to creep in and make my grief even worse.

We remember the last words or we have regrets about the words we didn't say. Did we hug them? Did we kiss them that last time? We fixate on the last moments often placing more importance of them than the years of joy we spent with them. We fixate on their moment of death and how they died. None of this is helpful. It's simply tormenting ourselves serving no good purpose. Grief is hard enough without guilt and regret. My advice is to let it go as soon as you possibly can.

# TRIGGERS

Grief can be punctuated by triggers. Triggers are events that cause an overwhelming flood of negative emotions such as terror, panic, or sadness. Anything can be a trigger- a song on the radio or an event such as a birthday or an anniversary. Some triggers are unavoidable. You can't get around a date on the calendar. Some are manageable, such as attending an event. You can choose to go or not go. You'll never be able to get away from all triggers. But, you can manage some and avoid others, until you're strong enough to deal with them.

Triggers can be managed by how you choose to look at them. Many people look at upcoming anniversaries, birthdays, and holidays with dread. I've chosen to look at dates like Christmas, birthdays, etc. as milestones. Rather than mourning the fact Shayna isn't here to share them with me, I focus on the fact that it means I've made it past another milestone. Every Christmas I put behind me is one less Christmas I have to spend without Shayna. Every year her birthday rolls around is evidence of my strength to survive.

Go through the grief. Triggers will be there. Manage them. Lean into them. There is nothing wrong with crying. Don't be embarrassed or try to avoid it.

A sunny day and listening to the radio was a trigger for me once on the way to see my grief counselor. I burst into tears in the car in the midst of enjoying the sun on my face and a favorite old song on the radio. Because Shayna wasn't there to enjoy the beautiful day and the way the music made me feel, I felt survivor's guilt. I didn't want to be happy. The act of driving past the Taco Bell, where Shayna and I shared memories, just the two of us, was another trigger. Triggers are impossible to avoid.

Some triggers I avoid entirely. Shayna's high school graduation would have been last year. There was no way I was going to the graduation ceremony even though I know they honored her there. I wasn't up to it. I didn't go to the graduation parties of the girls in her class. They were like sisters to Shayna and I love them. But, I wasn't up to going to their parties. So, I didn't. My niece, who is only a few months younger than Shayna had a graduation party. I had to attend. But, I had a plan to manage it. Before we left for the party, I made a deal with my wife that we would stay a specific amount of time. Knowing I had a time that I could escape helped me manage.

## FEAR

The loss of a loved one can lead to feelings of fear. The worst has already happened. You might think "Lightning can't strike twice." and be fine. Or you might think since the unspeakable and unthinkable has happened, it could happen again.

The telephone ringing may cause your heart to race as you anticipate more bad news. I still get a start when the telephone rings late at night or if my other daughter calls instead of texting. Your other child not answering text or phone call might send you into a tailspin. This happened to us once when Kayla overslept, for hours, in her dorm room in Toledo, almost three hours from where we live. We called and called as we made the drive to her college. We were on the way to pick her up that day. She was supposed to call us first thing to tell us what to bring. Tywana and I were both terrified as we made that drive. Separately, we thought "Should we call the police?", neither of us dared to speak it aloud. Finally, sleepily, she answered her phone, which had been on silent. PTSD had both of us spinning out of control, turning a typical teenage situation, oversleeping and having her phone on silent, into a perceived disaster.

Another fear that you may have is that you will die or that you won't die soon enough. Since your loved one died, you wonder if it will happen to you. Or, you might desire to be with them and fear that you will have a long life instead. This is particularly true for a parent whose child has gone first. We obsess. "Who is there taking care of them? Will they grow up without me and I'll miss it? How long will I have to endure this pain? Will I forget her? Will she forget me? Will I forget the sound of his voice?" I sometimes sit and try to remember what Shayna's voice sounded like.

It's been almost four years since I heard her call me "Daddy". I wonder how much longer it will be. Fear of losing memory of her comes up sometimes and I have to remind myself I remember my grandmother who passed on over thirty years ago. I'll remember Shayna.

# CHAPTER 5
## WE GRIEVE BECAUSE WE LOVE

Consider this. If we didn't love, we wouldn't grieve. Your grief is a sign of your love. Your love didn't die when your loved one's body died. Love endures. The evidence of the survival of love is grief. Be grateful for the love that continues even though that love means you are now in pain.

I have a pair of sneakers with a graphic saying "Love is a gamble." I bought them years ago. I had no idea of the depth of meaning of that phrase until Shayna passed. My love for her was a tremendous gamble. Grief is the price we pay for love.

The more we love, the more crippling the pain can be. This doesn't mean if you love someone tremendously, you will never be able to get "over" the grief. It doesn't mean the longer you're unable to function after their death the more you loved them. You can and will learn to cope with the pain. Your love for them, and knowing they still love you and want the best for you, can help pull you out of those darkest days. You continue for them, as well as for yourself.

Grief feels like it will never end. Almost four years in, I don't think my grief will ever end. And, I'm OK with that. If grief is defined as missing them and wanting themback with us, for most of us, it will never end. Grief may lessen. It will lessen if you let it. Grief is like a chronic, incurable illness. It's not terminal. It will feel that way at times. You will learn to live with it.

When someone dies, for the survivor, serotonin levels dip to levels that make it difficult to function. The body may go into shock. During the grieving process, the brain uses serotonin faster than the body can make it. We are physically impacted as well as emotionally.

With low serotonin levels, our sleep is off. We may sleep too much. Maybe we can't sleep at all. Concentration and attention are difficult. We misplace things. We lose physical energy. We are tired. Sexual interest may drop. We may eat too much or not enough. Interest in social interaction may wane causing us to isolate ourselves. Solitude can be a good thing. It gives us time to process. However, too much isolation may lead to loneliness which can exacerbate grief.

Grief is a natural state. Or, is it? I think at the heart of grief is the belief, conscious or subconscious, that this is the end. I go back to the example of a loved one on a long trip. We miss them. We don't grieve them. We don't grieve because we have a virtual certainty they will return.

Faith can undoubtedly help with grief. But, even the most devout people have some amount of doubt. At least a part of us believes we will never see our loved one again. A part of us tells us they are gone. They have disappeared from existence. As much as we might hope for the existence of heaven, we don't know for sure. Even given signs or even after death communications via a medium, dream visits, or some other vehicle, we still have some skepticism. The greater the doubt, the more intense and consuming the grief.

Emmanuel Swedenborg, an 18th-century mystic, theologian and all-around Renaissance man had special revelations from angels and spirits throughout the last few decades of his life. He said it was revealed to him there was a time in man's history where we conversed freely with spirits, including the souls of departed loved ones. The veil between here and there was very thin.

As we "evolved," we have evolved to a state where the veil has grown increasingly thick because modern humans do a lot more thinking than feeling. I believe the veil between us and those who have gone before has become so thick that we, as a species, have completely forgotten who we are. This state leads us to grieve in ways that I don't believe was intended for us.

Many say the veil is now growing thinner. Perhaps it has peaked. Materialism seems to be on the wane. Scientific breakthroughs are showing us the ancient mystics were right about many things modern man has forgotten. Science is catching up with what was faith. I hope that one day we'll get to the point where grief is no worse than missing a child who has gone off to college or a friend who has moved to a different country. I intend to do my part to get us there. The closer we get to knowing our loved one is no more than a thought away now and that we will see them again "soon", the better we can cope with grief.

# Chapter 6
## Grief is not an illness

Grief is an inevitable part of life. Some think there is a cure for grief and they treat grief like a disease.

Grief counseling may or may not be beneficial to you. Most people are able to deal with most grief with their social network of family and friends. If you're functioning normally, able to get out of bed, sleep, work, etc., you might not need grief counseling. However, if you're having suicidal thoughts, can't sleep, can't eat, you require medical intervention. If there is any doubt, get to your doctor. Some red flags are: Your mind speeds up. Your brain fixates on bad things. Your thoughts torture you. You think you're a burden. You start to believe that no one cares about you. You're convinced your family would be better off without you. You think you would be better off dead. You contemplate violence against yourself. SEE YOUR DOCTOR. You may even need medication.

# IS COUNSELING NECESSARY OR EVEN DESIRABLE?

Studies have shown that grief counseling is less beneficial than other types of mental health counseling. I don't say that to discourage you from getting counseling. It can be quite beneficial. It's likely the studies show grief counseling to be less beneficial because, for most grief, grief is something that people naturally progress through. Grief counseling must be necessary and done at the proper time to have a positive impact. In some cases, grief counseling can even have a negative impact. This is particularly true with men. The message here is "Do what works for you."

Grief counseling is normally indicated in "complicated grief" which would include trauma (for example witnessing a horrific scene of a death), the loss of a child, or guilt associated with the passing of someone. If your 100-year-old grandma dies a natural death in her bed, chances are you will be able to deal with it on your own. If your child completes suicide, that might be a completely different story that demands some help.

Counseling can be providing a listening ear and nothing more. Friends can provide this.

Counselors cannot "fix" you, but they are trained listeners, and you might not feel as "needy" talking to someone you are paying to listen, rather than "burdening" friends and family. Also, counselors are not going through the grieving process like a friend or family may be with you. If your friend shared a special relationship with your loved one, they might not be in a position to help you while they are grieving themselves. When you are with a counselor, you can comfortably focus on you because that is what the counselor is being paid to do.

## THE MYTH OF THE FIVE STAGES OF GRIEF

Elizabeth Kubler-Ross' famous five stages of death are stages of acceptance of death by the dying. They were never intended to describe to the grief process. Applying these stages to grief is a common mistake, even among many grief counselors. Misapplication of these stages can be harmful, setting people up to think their grief will have an orderly linear progression. Your grief process will be unique. You may or not go through these stages.

Grief will most likely be a part of your life, in one way or another, for the rest of your life. The pain may or may not subside. It almost certainly will become more bearable. Some say it recedes. I think this is a matter of perception. I believe for most of us what happens is we will learn to live with it. We make room for it. Our capacity to carry the pain increases. When you are weight lifting, a twenty-five-pound weight always weighs twenty-five pounds. But, working out every day with that twenty-five-pound weight strengthens your muscles, making that weight seem lighter. You eventually lift it with ease.

Will grief last forever? The answer is yes, no, and it depends. My grandmother, who played a huge role in raising me from the time I was about seven years old, passed when I was in my early 20s. I suppressed my grief telling myself it was natural that she died and I didn't need to grieve her passing. I stuffed the grief away. I didn't even attend her funeral. It was about three years later, during a time of emotional turmoil that the pain finally surfaced and I dealt with it. But, I did deal with it, and I can say 35 years later I'm no longer grieving her. I miss her. I think of her fondly. I look forward to hugging her again when my time comes. But, I don't mourn her anymore.

On the other end of the spectrum, my 15-year-old daughter slipped away in her sleep four years ago. Her passing was sudden and unexpected. She went to bed and didn't wake up. I grieve her tremendously, every single day. She was not supposed to go before me. She was not supposed to go at fifteen. I'm dealing with PTSD because my wife and I found her. I fully expect to grieve her passing for the rest of my days.

# MOVING ON OR MOVING FORWARD

I often hear the phrase "moving on." The expectation to move on from the loss of a dear loved one, particularly one that is out of order, is inconceivable to me. I can't move on. In fact, I don't want to move on. That implies that I leave the life of my loved one in the past never to have her as part of my life again. I don't move on from grief, I move forward with grief. I fully believe that when we depart from this plane, it's only our body that dies. Our spirit continues. My daughter will be a part of my life for the remainder of the time I walk the Earth. I will carry her with me. I will take the grief with me until we are together again. Then, and only then, will the grief end. And that is OK. Grief is part of being human.

# CHAPTER 7
## WHAT YOU CAN DO ABOUT GRIEF
## TAKE IT HEAD ON

Blocking grief does not solve the problem. Choosing to ignore grief delays its expression and can make it worse. Grief must be dealt with. How you deal with grief is up to you. Some will choose to try to ignore their grief, burying themselves in work, or drinking. These are temporary measures that will only delay the grieving process.

Grief is physical. It is exhausting. Grief uses a lot of energy. It is difficult to do anything else while we are grieving. While we are mourning we also have to maintain relationships, work, take care of family, and meet the other demands of life.

I recently read of a mother who returned to work after the passing of her daughter. Her co-workers reported that she was "too sad" and should be sent home. Her boss called her into the office and tried to get her to take more time off. She could not afford to take more time off. He offered short-term disability, at a reduced salary. She could not afford to work for less money. As grieving people, we are often put into seemingly impossible situations which adds stress to the grief. The world expects us to carry on with worldly responsibilities when often it is all we can do to keep breathing. Stress coping mechanisms will be necessary, in addition to coping with grief.

Relying on your family may be difficult. They might not be able to be there for you because they too are grieving and need all of their energy for themselves. You may need to rely on people outside of the family, temporarily. A friend with some distance from your loved one who has passed, a grief counselor, a pastor, or a life coach can be helpful.

However, relationships can grow stronger during grief if you honor each others' pain without judgment and face it together. When it comes to those closest to us, we can either grow together or grow apart.

There is a myth that when a married couple loses a child, divorce is almost inevitable. There is a belief that as many as 90% of couples whose children pass end up divorcing. This was cited in a book titled "The Bereaved Parent". The myth spread like wildfire until it became an accepted fact that a well meaning friend informed me of weeks after Shayna's passing. I'm happy to report there is no data to support this myth.

When Shayna passed, I was fortunate. Tywana jumped with me right into the deep end of dealing with this. I had been meditating for years. I had been studying the afterlife for over a dozen years. Tywana wasn't interested in any of it before. But, we faced our grief together. She began reading the books I was reading. She started meditating. She listened to the podcasts I listened to. We discussed those things together. She was the one who proposed we attend a more after-life focused church. We left the soulless megachurch we had been going to, and we started going to a small Unity church. Throughout this process, facing it together has kept us together.

## SELF CARE

The number one thing with grief, especially in the early days, is to take care of yourself. This is a time when you will need to nurture yourself to survive. Here are a few things you can do to take care of yourself- meditation, podcasts, books (possibly audiobooks because you might not be able to concentrate on reading), friends, grief counseling, rituals, exercise, avoid self-medication (excessive alcohol), write/journal, record audio, volunteer-helping others takes your mind off of yourself. Twenty minutes of exercise in the sunshine is a fantastic natural antidepressant. Eat right. Find groups like Helping Parents Heal. Don't isolate yourself. I list these in particular because I did all of the above.

When Shayna passed, I was already walking every day. I added a couple of miles to my daily walk. I started listening to podcasts and/or music that either uplifted me or helped me express my grief. There is this strange human phenomenon. When we are down, it often helps to listen to music that conveys those same sentiments. In those early days, I found music that expressed profound loss helped me deal with the loss. It helped to know I wasn't the only one on the planet who ever had to deal with this. It was both cathartic and therapeutic. The tears that flowed while I listened allowed the emotion to flow through me rather than remain stuck in me.

Faith can help. If your religious tradition helps you, lean on it. If not, find something that does. Traditional belief might not be enough. Bearing down and trying to believe based on ancient texts might or might not work at this time. Examine the evidence. If you need more evidence, get it. Studying Near Death Experiences (NDEs), mediumship, afterlife communications can do wonders. Extensive reading about NDEs can have very similar impacts as having an NDE. Some religions will preclude these things. You'll need to ask yourself what is more important, obeying someone's idea of what you should or should not do or being healthy? If you feel anger, find a way to process it. Do vigorous yard work. Take a self-defense class. Punch pillows. Scream into a pillow. Find something (not valuable) you can destroy. Clearing brush helped me.

Try to develop good habits. Make meditation and/or exercise a routine. Get an app to make you accountable; something that will track your exercise and perhaps even remind you. Insight Timer and FitBit are a couple of the tools I use. Insight Timer is my meditation app. I started a challenge at the beginning of 2017 to meditate at least once a day for 365 days. When 2017 ended, and I completed the year meditating every day, I thought, "Why quit now?". I'm on day 886 as of the time of writing this. I use my Fitbit to encourage myself to get in 10,000 steps a day. The only way to ensure I get my steps is to get 10,000 steps in before I start work for the day. So, I take a walk of at least 10,000 steps first thing every morning. During that time, I listen to inspiring music or spiritual podcasts. There are dozens of podcasts that can help you cope with grief, understand where your loved ones are, lift your spirits, and get you through the day.

## Transform your grief

Many people find purpose out of their grief. If you're in the early stages, this will sound like complete nonsense to you. You are welcome to skip this part of the teaching. But, eventually, you may come to find purpose from your grief. You can volunteer to help people with the disease that caused your loved one's departure. You could eventually help other grieving people. I got help from a local grief organization, then from Helping Parents Heal. I quickly moved to become a leader in Helping Parents Heal, as part of my healing process. Giving back helps me. You could volunteer at an animal shelter. It doesn't have to be directly related to death/dying/disease. Anything that contributes to the legacy of your loved one and redeems their passing, even in a small way helps relieve a bit of the pain. Starting a scholarship fund or a memorial fund in your loved one's name helps keep their memory alive among other people.

# Practice Gratitude

Just trust me on this one. When I first heard I should be grateful, I thought "Are you insane? The worst thing possible just happened to me, and you want me to be grateful?" Hear me out. You're not going to be grateful for the death that has caused you to go into mourning. That's not what we are talking about.

We humans naturally focus on what is wrong rather than what is right. When the worst happens this is a perfect opportunity to do just that. You will be consumed with grief for a while, with no room for anything else. But, as soon as possible, find something to be grateful for. There is always something. You've heard "I cried because I had no shoes. Then, I met a man who had no feet." Be grateful for your feet. It might be something as small as the sunshine on a cold winter day or the smile of one of your children. Make it a regular practice. Some people keep a gratitude journal as a practice. When I wake up in the morning, before I get out of bed, I name three things I am grateful for that day. I try to make them unique, not repeating the same thing every day. This helps me focus my mind on the positive.

## PRACTICE FORGIVENESS

We tend to want to find someone to blame when something goes wrong. It might be the doctor who took care of our loved one and let her die. It might be the driver of the other car. We might blame our spouse. We might be angry with our loved one who is gone because he left us. We might even be angry with ourselves. Guilt can easily turn into self-hatred. The reality is we human beings are all doing the best we can, with the information we have, at the time we have it. Hindsight is always 20/20. I wondered whether the drugs we gave Shayna for her rheumatoid arthritis contributed to her death. Did I do something wrong with her injection two days before her heart stopped? Why didn't the cardiologist know her condition was life-threatening? I wanted to punch that guy in the face. When I had to face him again, I didn't want to hear his excuses. I didn't want to hear his apologies. I just wanted to be mad.

I quickly realized none of this would do anyone any good, most of all me. I trusted the doctors, and we did everything we could possibly do for Shayna. We treated the very minor heart condition we were told she had as aggressively as possible. She had two procedures. She was being monitored. She was cleared for sports by one of the best pediatric cardiologists in the country. I had to give her the medicine the doctors suggested for her arthritis because the arthritis was severe and would have been debilitating. Before the injections, she was in tremendous pain. The medicine put her into complete remission. I let go of any ill feelings towards her doctors and I refused to blame myself. I did what I had to do at the time.

Trusting that whatever happens is for our highest good and will ultimately work out that way means you have to forgive. If you can truly embrace this, you will be able to let go of any grudge against anyone, including yourself. It's easier said than done. But, it's well worth the effort.

## FIND HOPE

I could not endure without hope. I am a firm believer that human beings need confidence that life will get better, as much as we need food and water, to survive. If we don't see any possibility of a good future, what is the point of living? If you believe your loved one is gone "forever," it's going to be difficult to find any hope.

The Bible says that those who have faith do not mourn like those who have no hope. It's not that we don't mourn, we just mourn differently. If we have hope, we can endure anything.

Nietzsche declared, "A man who has a why can endure any how". I find that believing there is a purpose to everything that happens helps me have a why. That is what gives me the strength to get through. I found that faith based on the words of ancients in the Bible or other texts wasn't enough for me. My "faith" comes as the result of years of diligent study. If you need evidence, that's OK. Don't let anyone make you feel bad about it. The evidence is there. Go out and find it.

I no longer *believe* in an afterlife any more than I *believe* the sun will rise tomorrow. It's not a belief, it's a knowing. Based on experience including signs, studying after death communications, medium readings, and scientific evidence ranging from controlled studies to the mountains of data from Near Death Experiences, Shared Death Experiences, quantum mechanics, and philosophy, I know that materialism makes no sense and science is proving this to be true. This universe is more than the sum of its material parts. Consciousness came before the material; consciousness is fundamental to all that is (Max Planck- Nobel Prize winning physicist said this over 100 years ago).

We human beings are more than the meatsuits that we walk around in. I know that we are spiritual beings having a temporary human experience. That knowledge lets me know that my Shayna is not gone. She is still right here, probably sitting on the couch next to me critiquing my writing. She is merely in a form that the physical senses I've come to rely on so heavily can't sense.

We perceive less than 5% or 1% of all reality, depending on who you ask. What physicists call "dark matter" and "dark energy" make up over 95% of the universe. Our eyes can only see a small portion of the electromagnetic spectrum. Even on this plane, other creatures can see things we find to be invisible. Bees see into the ultraviolet light range. Dogs hear sounds we can't hear. Our ears can only hear a small piece of the range of sounds. Other creatures literally experience a world different from the one we are in. Beyond that, who knows what exists that we can't perceive?

This body filters out the vast majority of what exists. Our best scientific instruments can't sense over 95% of our universe. When I shed the filters of this body, I'll be able to perceive the greater reality that I know exists. This gives me the hope I need to carry on.

I've heard people say "I'll never see her again." Those words have never crossed my lips. I won't see Shayna with these eyes again. But, when these eyes close for the final time and my spiritual eyes open, I will see her again. This is what drives me forward. This is why I celebrate each passing day. I do my best to fill each day with as much good as I can. But, I know that each one brings me one day closer to that glorious day.

## FIND YOUR TRIBE

When disaster happens is often when we find out people's true character. And, we will find out just how much we might have in common with them. People you were very close to might start to avoid you. They will not understand what you are going through. Some will say you should be over it by now and ready to "move on". You will have to accept that some relationships will be different and some will even end. I had relationships that I had had for years drift apart until we are no longer in contact anymore.

On the other hand, you will find relationships with people you might not have been all that close to growing stronger as they reveal more of themselves to you because you are revealing more of yourself to them. I found out that people in my life shared some of my beliefs about the afterlife and I had no idea. I had known some of them for nearly twenty years. One of my daughter's best friend's mother drove carpool with Shayna and her daughter. I barely knew her. She started a scholarship fund in Shayna's name, and she and her husband are among our closest friends now.

Tywana and I left our evangelical church which wasn't doing much for either of us. We found a church that was more in line with my spiritual beliefs and what Tywana's became after Shayna's passing. Joining Helping Parents Heal was a lifesaver for both of us. It's a safe space for us to talk with people who understand what "normal" people would find to be crazy talk. As I said earlier, you might find yourself thinking about dying yourself or even taking your own life. You can't share this feeling with just anyone. But, among our tribe, when a parent says this, instead this of us telling them they shouldn't feel that way it's much more likely that that we respond with "Yes. I know. I've felt that way, too. And, I can't wait to go Home, myself." It's important to find people who will understand you when you say things that others just cannot understand.

# CHAPTER 8
## THREE KEYS IDEAS TO LIVING WITH GRIEF

I intentionally say "living with grief" versus getting over grief or defeating grief. I don't see grief as something to be fought. But, grief is something we can learn to live with. There are three key ideas that if you can grasp and embrace will help you deal with the grief you are experiencing.

## DEATH IS NOT THE END

Language is important. You will rarely hear me say that someone died. The reason I won't say that is because none of us dies. We so closely identify with the body that we have the mistaken belief that we are our bodies. Therefore, we think, when our body dies, we die. We think we came into existence at birth and we cease to exist at death. Maybe we have a soul and our soul goes on. This is simply not true.

It's more accurate to say you have a body. You are a soul. Your body is a lot like your car. It's a vehicle you use to get around. When you get out of your vehicle, you don't cease to exist. You move about differently.

While the body is necessary to interact on this plane, it's not needed for consciousness or existence. When people cross over to the other side, a common way they explain the experience is "I just woke up.". The reports are that we feel more alive than ever when our bodies die. Death is not the end; it's a new beginning. When your loved one "died" they didn't cease to exist, not even for a moment. They moved on to a different plane of existence. A more vibrant, more "real" plane of existence, by the way. It's a plane of existence that makes this seem like a dream.

## YOU WILL SEE HER AGAIN

A common phrase among the grieving is "I'll never see her again." This belief is also inaccurate and unuseful. What you mean is your physical eyes will never see her physical presence again. That is very true.

Eventually, all of us have our moment to make our transition. We are not damned to live in these physical bodies forever. There will come a day that you will see her again. You will have a joyous reunion. And, on that day, the time that was in between will seem like only a moment. It will be a quickly fading memory.

What you need to hold onto today is that this day is another one along the road to that reunion. When you close your eyes tonight, you will be one day closer. I count down the days until that reunion takes place. That hope gets me through the day.

## She Didn't Go Anywhere

We tend to think of the "dead" as either asleep or in some far off place. They are gone. My studies show otherwise. Those who have crossed the veil are very much interested in and involved in our lives. We are a very real presence for them, right now. There are here guiding us. They send us signs. They are coordinating synchronicities.

I hear from Shayna regularly in various ways through all kinds of people and events. Intentionally, Shayna remains a part of my daily life. I wake up each day and tell her good morning. I tell her good night every night. There are photographs of her all over the house. Every morning, as I leave my bedroom, the first thing I see is a large photograph on canvas hanging on the wall. I greet her as I start down the stairs to face the day.

While it's not the same as having her physical presence, acknowledging Shayna's presence in my daily life helps me to remember points one and two in this section. Death was not the end of Shayna, and I will see her again.

# CHAPTER 9
## WHAT NOT TO SAY TO SOMEONE GRIEVING

We are all awkward around those who are grieving, even if we are grievers ourselves. We don't know the right thing to say.

Before we get to what not to say, know this. Grievers need to talk. They may repeat themselves. They are not looking for a response. They are not seeking to be fixed. They want a welcoming ear. As the person offering sympathy, we don't want to say the wrong thing. So, often we say nothing at all. If you don't know what to say, a simple "I don't know what to say." is always appropriate. When you do speak, focus on the one grieving.

Do not say "God needed another angel." This makes God selfish. Why would God need your loved one more than you do?

Do not say "Please let me know if there is anything I can do for you." is not very useful. I find myself saying this. Of course, it's well-intentioned. Especially in those early stages, grievers don't know what they need. Instead, offer something specific. Offer to prepare a meal. Take them out to lunch. Offer to watch their kids. Offer to clean the house.

Always useful is "I'm here to listen." Avoid "How are you doing?" The truth is they're doing awful. By asking how they're doing, you're putting them in a situation where they feel selfish or needy, or they are forced to lie. I catch myself saying this because it's such a common phrase in our society. Instead, say "I know it's tough for you right now."

Don't say "I know they're in a better place." Maybe the griever believes this; maybe he doesn't. But, you're assuming. Also, you're focusing on the departed rather than the griever. Try to focus on the griever. Instead, say "I'm sorry you have to go through this." Acknowledge the pain of the griever.

Never talk about a replacement "You can have another child." or "You're young, you can remarry." are like nails on a chalkboard. People are unique, one relationship does not replace another. Pointing out they have other children is also not helpful. Instead, engage them in conversation about their loved one. Grievers love to talk about their loved ones. Remember the special times. Honor the unique place of that loved one in the griever's life.

"I know how you feel." is something that we should normally avoid. Now that I have a child in spirit, I say this to other Shining Light Parents. I don't say it to anyone else. I have a special connection with them. However, I don't expect anyone who hasn't lost a child to say it to me. Instead, say "I'm trying to imagine how you feel." Empathize without assuming you know.

Don't say "You're handling this better than expected." While this seems like a compliment, the truth is the person is probably hiding most of their grief from you and probably feels like they're barely hanging on. Saying this doesn't permit them to express how they are truly feeling and could inadvertently make them feel like they have to keep up a strong front. Instead, say "I know this sucks and I know it's hard."

# Chapter 10
## My Grief Program

People like a program, step-by-step instructions for how to get something done. At least the engineer in me does. The reality is your grief journey will be yours uniquely. Part of the growth that will come will be due to you figuring it out and developing confidence in yourself. That does not mean we can't look for help along the way and learn from what does and does not work for others.

I've covered much of this already. However, here I offer a summary.

## Start with Gratitude

I resisted this. I looked into positive thinking years ago and found it to be nonsense. How is gratitude going to help? There are two ways, one is undeniable. The other you might debate. Gratitude raises our attitude/vibration by focusing us on what we have rather than what we don't have. That has an immediate impact. Some say we manifest our own reality and that gratitude is a first step to creating better circumstances. That's debatable. But, hey, being grateful can't hurt. However, gratitude isn't pretending that we don't have problems. Gratitude is a matter of focus. All of life is a mixture of good and bad. When we practice being grateful, we focus on what is going right at least as much as what is going wrong. I started with meditations that include affirmations. This helped me to be more receptive. When I say start with gratitude, I mean that quite literally. Every day before I get out of bed, I find three things to be grateful for. This takes a couple of minutes. Still, my first thought in the morning is "Damn! I'm here again?" Maybe that will change one day. But, right after that, I say "What are the three things I'm going to be grateful for today?" I try not to repeat. Everyday I try to find something novel. It might be that the weather's going to be nice. It might be that I have great friends. It might be that we're going out to dinner that night.

## EXERCISE

If I get regular exercise, I have more energy and I feel better. I have a Fitbit and my goal is 10,000 steps a day which is pretty aggressive, for someone who sits at a computer all day. Since I work from home, there are days, sometimes several in a row, when I don't leave the house. So, I start each day with a walk. When Shayna passed I was walking three to five miles a day most days. Now, I walk seven miles every morning. That's approximately 11,000 steps. By starting my day with that, I ensure I'll hit my step goal for the day. You might not be able to exercise first thing in the morning. But, maybe at lunchtime, you can eat for a few minutes and walk the building for half an hour. Or, you could take a long stroll after dinner.

## FEED MY MIND

I'm a politics junkie. So, some of the time when I'm walking I'm listening to political podcasts. But, I mostly listen to uplifting music or to spiritual podcasts. There is an abundance of podcasts that will reinforce the things I have chosen to believe- that we are spiritual creatures having a temporary human experience, that our loved ones are still with us, that we are going Home eventually, and that we have a job to do while we are here. This view is counter to modern culture. So, it is absolutely necessary for me to bolster this belief on a regular basis.

## MEDITATION

If I don't do it first thing in the morning, after I've gotten the urgent tasks of the day done, I meditate. I started at 5, then 10, then 15 minutes. I typically meditate for 30 minutes at a time now. I use Insight Timer and sit at my meditation altar which is has items that are sacred to me. I switch it up from listening to music, to listening to guided meditations, to listening to ambient sounds (to block any background noise). I don't get the great out of body, life-changing experiences some people get in meditation. But, I find meditation helps me slow my mind even when I'm not on the cushion. It gives me mental discipline and clarity. I think it allows me to connect with Shayna. Meditation has gone from being a chore when I started to something I look forward to.

## SERVICE

One of the best ways to heal is by helping others. I was fortunate enough to find Helping Parents Heal through a series of synchronous events. Being a leader in Helping Parents Heal is healing for me. I look to the parents who have more time in than I do as inspiration. I look at the new ones just coming in, and I can see how far I've come. Shayna pushes me to do more and I accept the challenge. She's constantly on me to write more, to finish that course, to reach out to that person. Service to others brings a sense of purpose, which brings a sense of fulfillment, which brings joy. I volunteer at my church. I volunteer on the SoulPhone project and a venture called Greater Reality Living. These give my life purpose and meaning and help pass the time until I rejoin Shayna.

## READING

I don't read as much as I'd like to. I typically end my day with fifteen to thirty minutes of reading. My material is something about the nature of reality or the afterlife mostly. I read very little fiction not because I don't like it. I don't have the time. The more I know, the more confident I am in the worldview that allows me to survive. So, I read about NDEs, afterlife communications, the latest scientific discoveries about human nature and the nature of the universe, spirituality, anything that helps me improve myself and understand more.

# CHAPTER 11
## SUMMARY

Grief can come out of nowhere, as it did for me. Or, grief might announce itself through a prolonged terminal illness. Either way, grief is an unwelcome stranger when it enters our life. It will feel, relentless, unending, and unyielding. It comes in waves and strikes at the worst times. We will feel like we have been buried, never to see the sun or feel warmth again. As long as we maintain hope, these things are not true. These are lies grief whispers in our ears.

We can overcome grief. We can transmute it. We can make grief serve us. We have been planted, not buried.

We can become better, stronger people as a result of having endured. The soil that buried us and once seemed cold and suffocating begins to warm. We pull in strength from around us. We put down roots and push upward, eventually breaking through to see the sun is still shining. And we grow and produce fruit again.

We are stronger than we know. We are more resilient than we know. These things that beat on us prompt us to grow and become stronger. What we need to survive is already within us. Trust that you will bring it forth when it's needed.

# CHAPTER 12
## WANT TO KNOW MORE?

You can find me at www.grief2growth.com . That is my life coaching business site and I have a blog there. You can email me at brian@grief2growth.com. Helping Parents Heal at www.helpingparentsheal.org is an invaluable resource for parents whose children have passed on. The blog I started after Shayna transitioned is at www.shaynaelayne.com That blog is a combination of a diary of my grief journey and observations and things I have learned along the way.

I'm a life coach and small business consultant. You can schedule a free half hour consultation with me on my website.

BRIAN D. SMITH

# NOTES

# NOTES

# NOTES

# NOTES

# NOTES

# NOTES

# NOTES

# NOTES

# NOTES

# NOTES

# NOTES

_____

_____

_____

_____

_____

_____

_____

_____

_____

_____

_____

_____

_____

_____

_____

_____

_____

_____

_____

_____

_____

# NOTES

# NOTES

_____

_____

_____

_____

_____

_____

_____

_____

_____

_____

_____

_____

_____

_____

_____

_____

_____

_____

_____

_____

_____

# NOTES

# NOTES

# NOTES

# NOTES

# NOTES

# NOTES

# NOTES

# NOTES

# NOTES

Made in the USA
Middletown, DE
10 April 2022

63978128R00061